AARON JAY KERNIS

TWO SONGS:
Love and Spirit

FOR VOICE AND PIANO

T0070716

AMP 8304
First Printing: February 2016

ISBN: 978-1-4950-6113-4

AJK Music
ADMINISTERED EXCLUSIVELY BY
Associated Music Publishers, Inc.
DISTRIBUTED BY
HAL•LEONARD®

Love

Treasure a love that burns so fine
It defies the rule and passage of time;
Deeper than the sea, softer than a song,
Desire sees no fault in rapture sublime.

Like a single white star emerging at night
In the vastness of an immortal joy,
The dream will survive in eternal love,
No human error or death may destroy.

Pure silken threads lace the heavens' line
In homage to the dying crimson sun;
And the light carries the heart beyond all grief
To a love, undenied, two souls as one.

Spirit

On a night when the course
of life is run,
And the heart and the light
at last entwine,
The beauty of all the world
now unfolds
In breathless grace only
faith may define.

In this instant's bliss,
when innocence thrives,
And stars hang so low as
to touch the heart,
The soul may arise to
reach the divine,
Leaving imprints on earth
as works of art.

At the hour when planets
halt in their path,
To receive the noble and sinner
as one;
The truth of a fortune,
dismal or fine,
Matters not when Heaven's
kindness is won.

Poems from *Beloved Spirit: Pathways to Love, Grace and Mercy* by Alexandra Villard de Borchgrave.
Reproduced by permission of the Light of Healing Hope Foundation,
2801 New Mexico Avenue, N.W., Suite 1224, Washington, DC 20007

Information on Aaron Jay Kernis and his works is available at www.musicsalesclassical.com

Commissioned by the Light of Healing Hope Foundation in memory
of those who were lost on September 11, 2001.

Two Songs: Love and Spirit

Alexandra Villard De Borchgrave

Aaron Jay Kernis
(2011)

1. Love

Slowly, supple ♩ = 42

Soprano

Piano

p, espr.

mp

Ped.

pp

Trea -

poco f *mp* *p* *mf* *mf*

p

sure   a   love   that   burns_____   so   fine_____

p

espr.

p

mf

It de-fies the rule_____ and pas-sage of

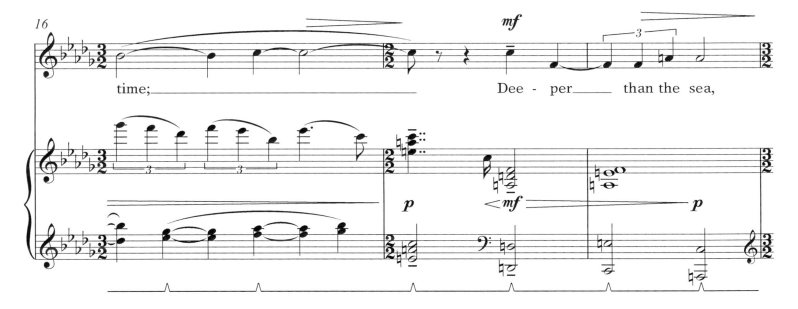

time;_____ Dee - per_____ than the sea,

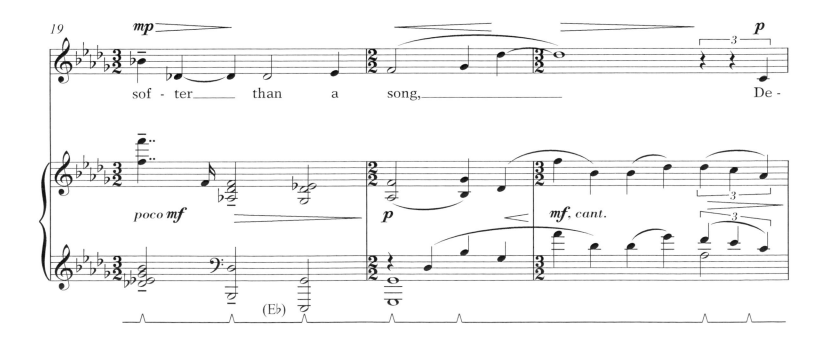

sof - ter_____ than a song,_____ De-

sire_____ sees no fault_____ in rap - ture sub -

lime._____

**Tempo 1,
a little quicker**

Like a sin - gle white star___ e -mer - ging___ at night___

use Ped. for legato
mp, espr.

in the vast - - ness__ of an im-

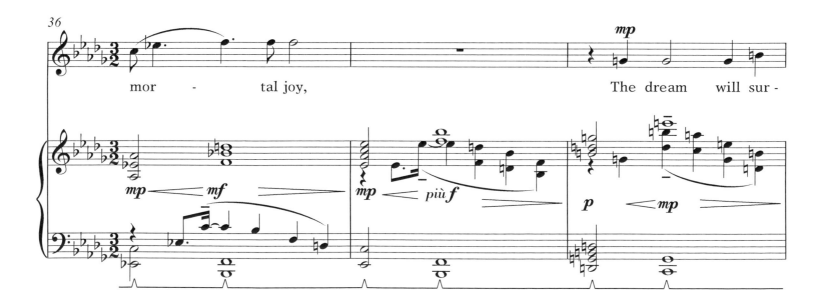

mor - tal joy, The dream will sur -

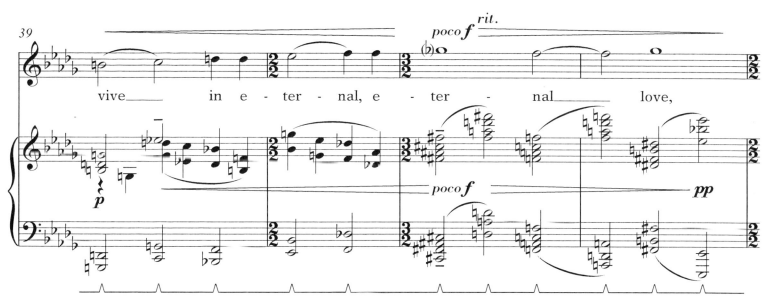

vive_____ in e - ter - nal, e - ter - nal_____ love,

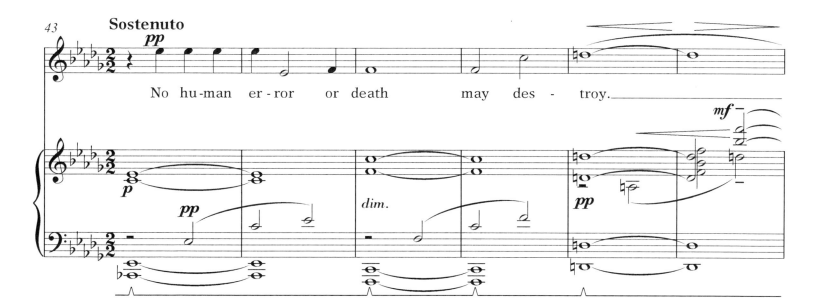

No hu-man er - ror or death may des - troy._____

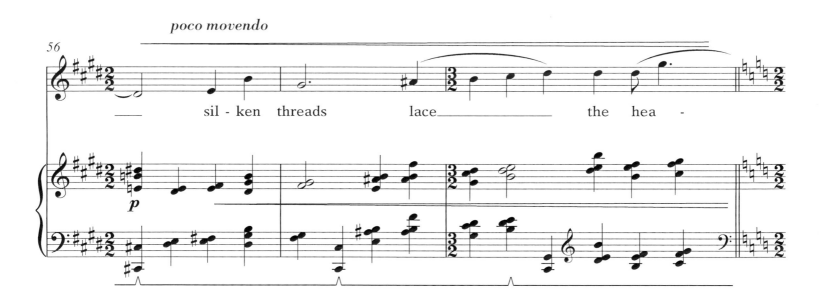

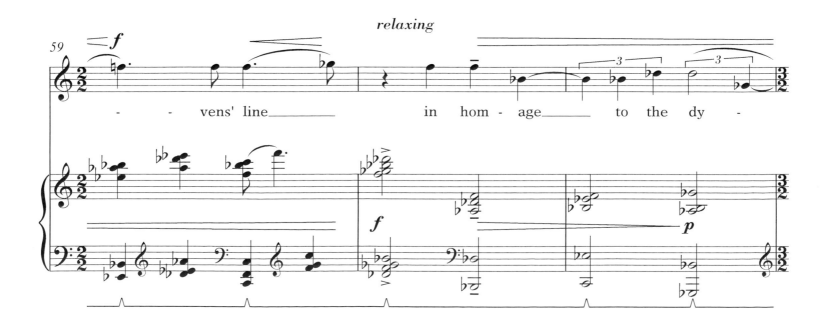

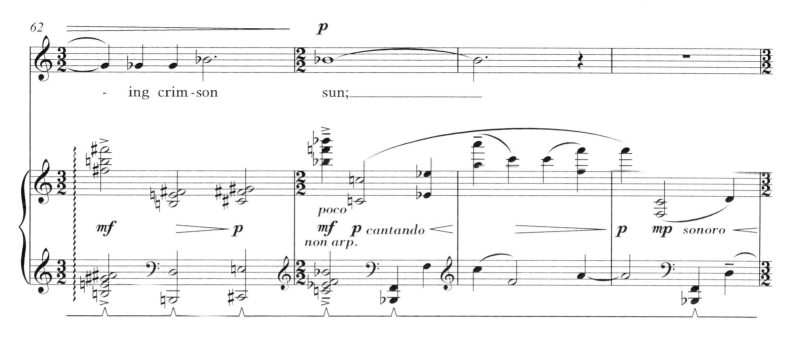

- ing crim-son sun;

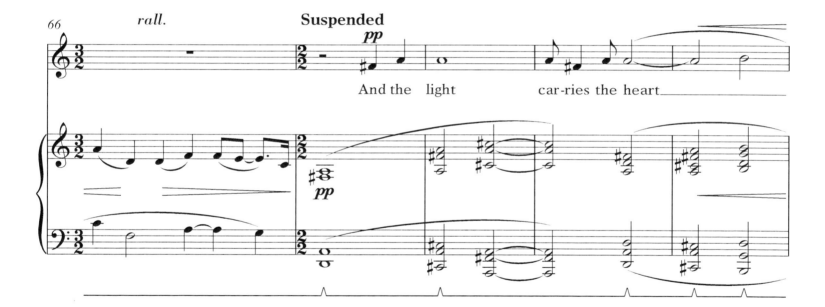

And the light car-ries the heart

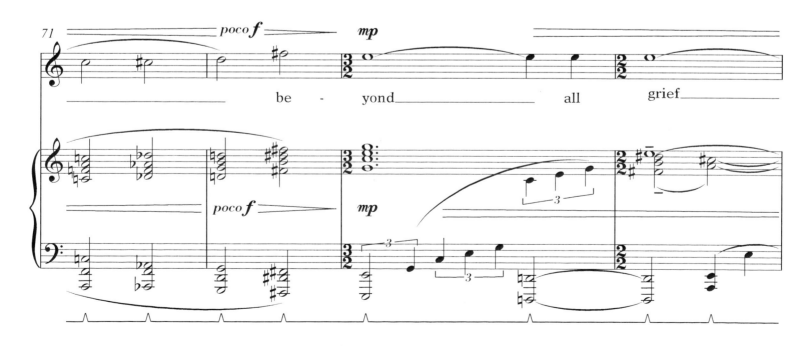

be - yond all grief

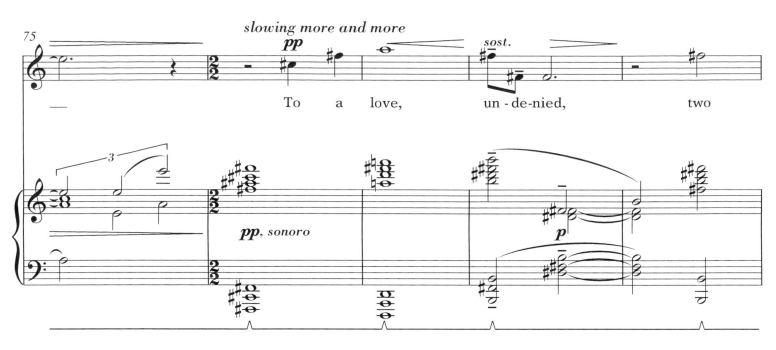

slowing more and more

To a love, un-de-nied, two

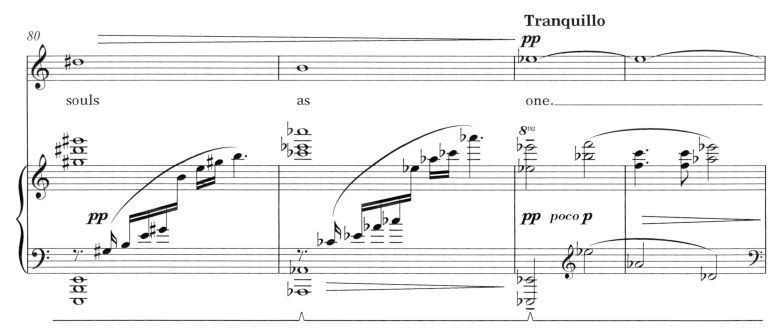

souls as one.

Tranquillo

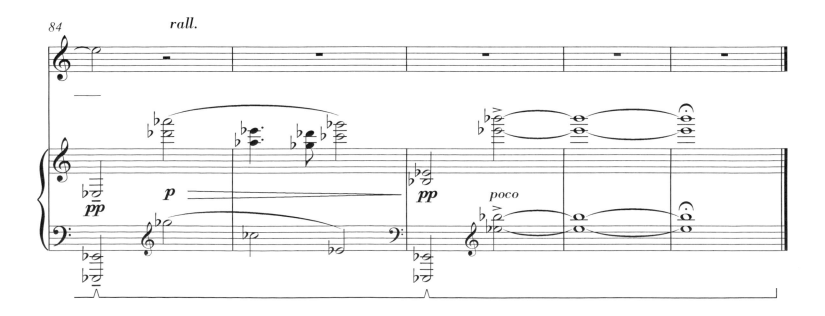

rall.

2. Spirit

Alexandra Villard De Borchgrave

Aaron Jay Kernis
(2011)

10

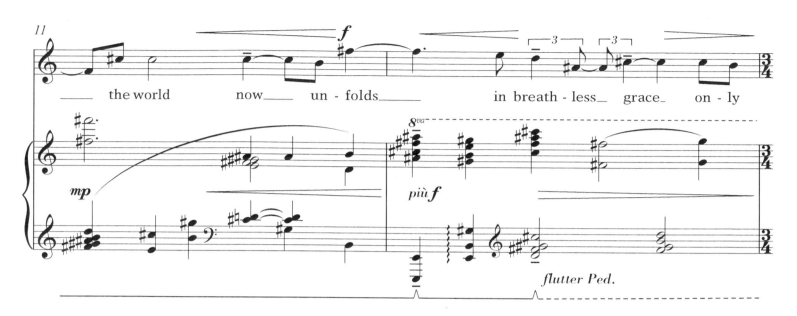

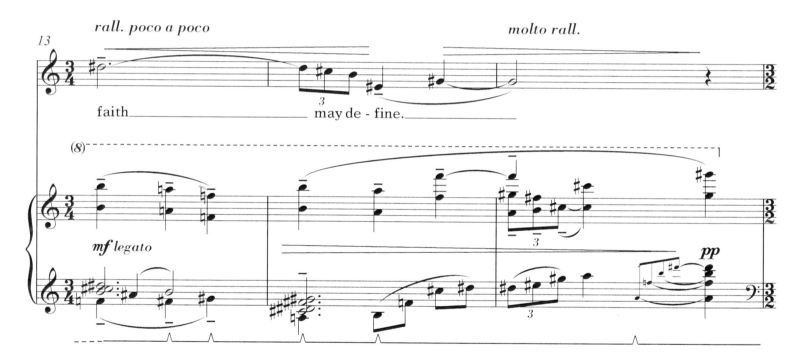

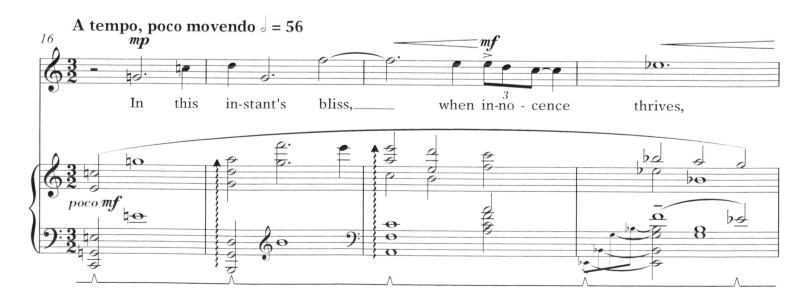

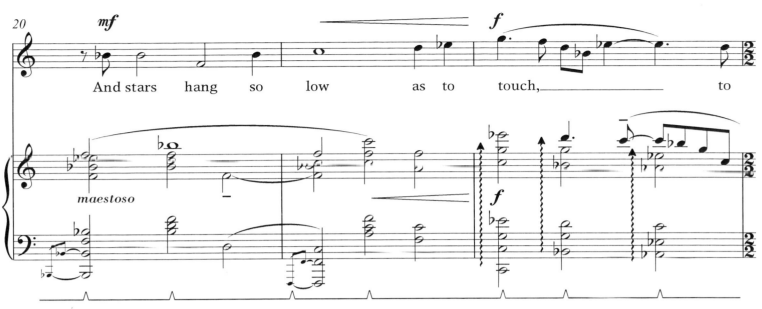

add Sost. Ped. as needed

Suddenly turbulent

Passionate, not rushed ♩ = 52

The soul_____ may a - rise,_____

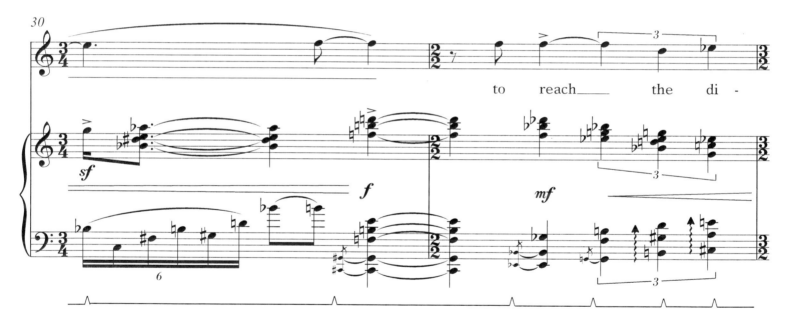

to reach_____ the di -

poco allarg.

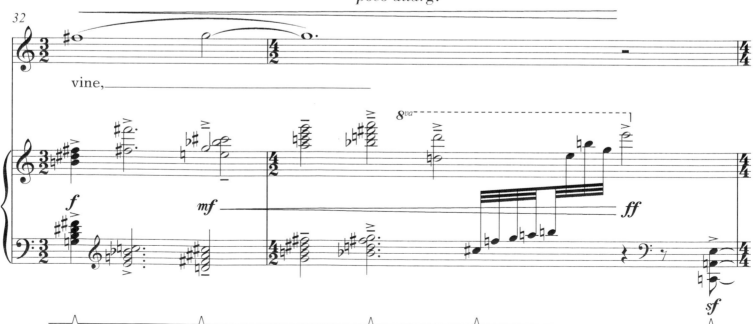

vine,_____

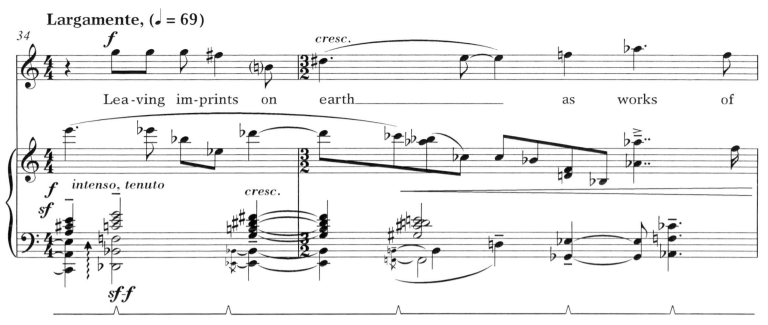

Lea-ving im-prints on earth_____ as works of

one,   as   one;

rit. **Molto sostenuto**
p, sotto voce

The   truth   of   a   for-tune,   dis - mal   or

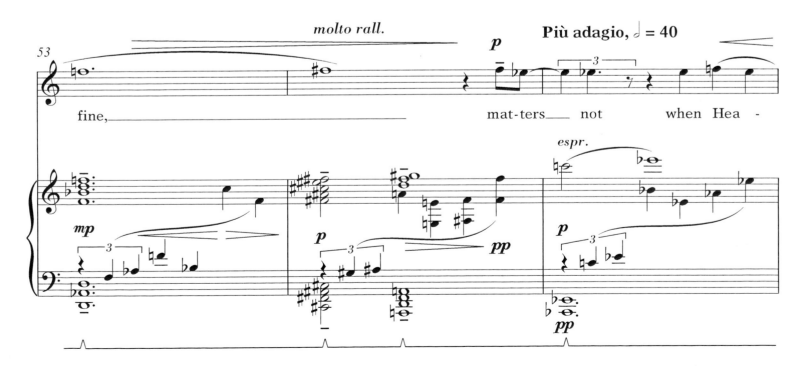

molto rall.   *p*   **Più adagio,** ♩ = 40

fine,_____   mat-ters____ not   when Hea -

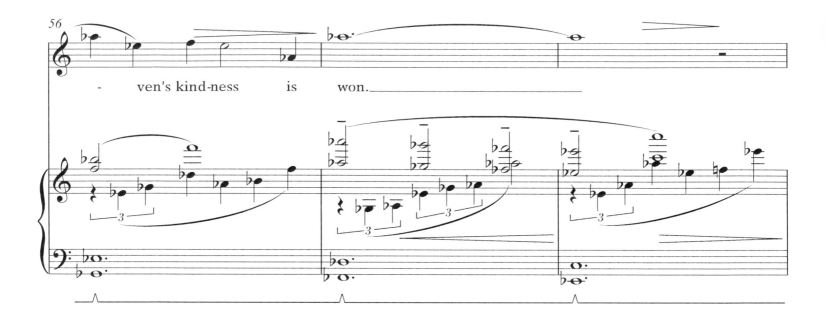

- ven's kind-ness   is   won._____

(D♭)

Tranquillo *allarg.*

dim.

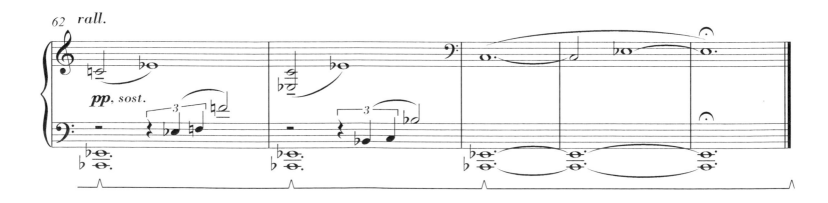

62 rall.

pp, *sost.*